I0566523

S⦿nar and Submarine Technology

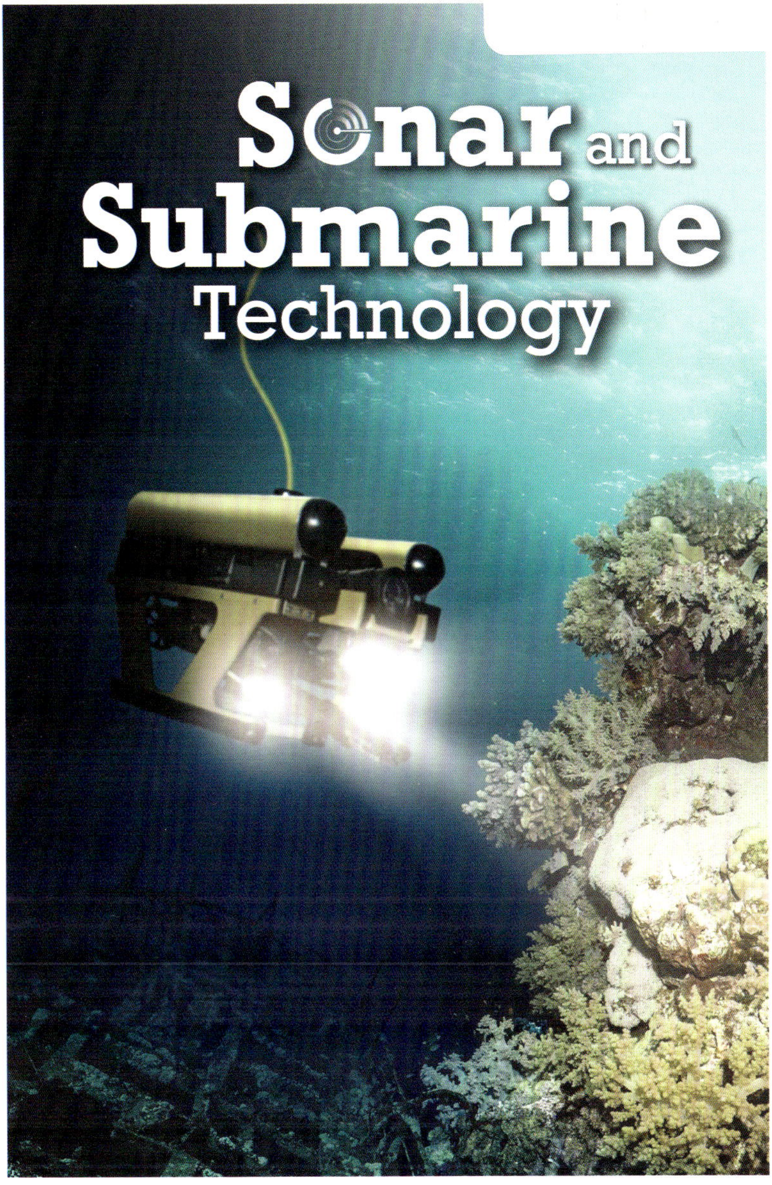

Eric Braun, M.F.A.

Consultants

Dr. Aaron O'Dea
Staff Scientist
Smithsonian Tropical Research Institute

Cheryl Lane, M.Ed.
Seventh Grade Science Teacher
Chino Valley Unified School District

Michelle Wertman, M.S.Ed.
Literacy Specialist
New York City Public Schools

Publishing Credits

Rachelle Cracchiolo, M.S.Ed., *Publisher*
Emily R. Smith, M.A.Ed., *SVP of Content Development*
Véronique Bos, *VP of Creative*
Dani Neiley, *Editor*
Robin Erickson, *Senior Art Director*
Kevin Pham, *Senior Graphic Designer*

Smithsonian Enterprises

Avery Naughton, *Licensing Coordinator*
Paige Towler, *Editorial Lead*
Jill Corcoran, *Senior Director, Licensed Publishing*
Brigid Ferraro, *Vice President of New Business and Licensing*
Carol LeBlanc, *President*

Image Credits: p.4 NOAA; p.5 (middle and bottom) NOAA; p.7
(top) MediaNews Group/The Mercury News via Getty Images; p.7
(middle) NOAA; p.8 Homer Sykes /Alamy Stock Photo; p.9 (middle)
James MacDonald/Bloomberg via Getty Images; p.10 (middle and
bottom) NOAA; p.11 (top) Imeh Akpanudosen/Getty Images; p.11
(bottom) Art Howard/NOAA; p.12 (bottom) Bettmann/Getty Images;
 p.13 (top and bottom) NOAA; p.14 Deb Gochfeld/NOAA; p.15 all images
NOAA; p.16 NOAA; p.17 (top) NOAA; p.27 (top and middle) NOAA; p.32 NOAA;
all other images from Shutterstock and/or iStock

Library of Congress Cataloging in Publication Control Number: 2024033346

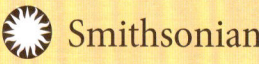

5482 Argosy Avenue
Huntington Beach, CA 92649
www.tcmpub.com
ISBN 979-8-7659-6879-6
© 2025 Teacher Created Materials, Inc.
Printed by: 51497
Printed in: China

© 2025 Smithsonian Institution. The name "Smithsonian" and
the Smithsonian logo are registered trademarks owned by the
Smithsonian Institution.

This book may not be reproduced or distributed in any way without
prior written consent from the publisher.

Table of Contents

The Darkest World

Imagine that you are a **marine** biologist. You want to learn about underwater life and see what the seafloor looks like. So, you put on your wet suit and plunge into the icy waters to look around. But there's just one problem. As you sink, it gets darker and darker, until you can't see your hand in front of your face! How are you supposed to study the plants and wildlife if you can't even see them?

The answer is a type of technology called *sonar*. Scientists all over the world use sonar to learn about what they can't see with their own eyes. First, they send sound waves into the water. When the sound waves hit an object in the water or on the ocean floor, they bounce back. Computers record the bounces and produce a video or image that scientists can study. This allows scientists to identify fish and mammal species and track their movements and sizes. Scientists can also learn about predator and prey interactions.

Submarines allow scientists to study deep-sea corals.

Sonar can be **deployed** from different vessels, such as boats or **submarines**. When sonar is combined with submarine technology, it allows scientists to unlock many secrets of our oceans. For example, sonar and submarines have been used to map the seafloor, study deep-sea **corals**, and examine how humans affect whales.

Scientists prepare to launch a submarine that will map the oceans.

This sonar map shows an undersea volcano with the highest points in warm colors and the lowest points in cool colors.

Take a Deep Dive

You may know that oceans cover more than two-thirds of Earth's surface. But did you know that they make up about 95 percent of Earth's living space? That's because they're so deep. A vast and mysterious world lies beneath the oceans. Humans have only been able to explore a very tiny part of it.

It's easy to see why most of the oceans have gone unexplored. Near the surface, some sunlight penetrates the water. But go deeper, and the light quickly begins to fade. The deepest that light has been seen is 700 meters (2,297 feet). Go deeper still, and the pressure of the water is a massive force. It takes great protective measures to withstand that force. The average depth of the oceans is 3,729 m (12,234 ft.). The water here is colder than the temperature of your refrigerator. The deepest parts of the oceans are more than 10,973 m (36,000 ft.) below the surface. That's almost 11 kilometers (7 miles)!

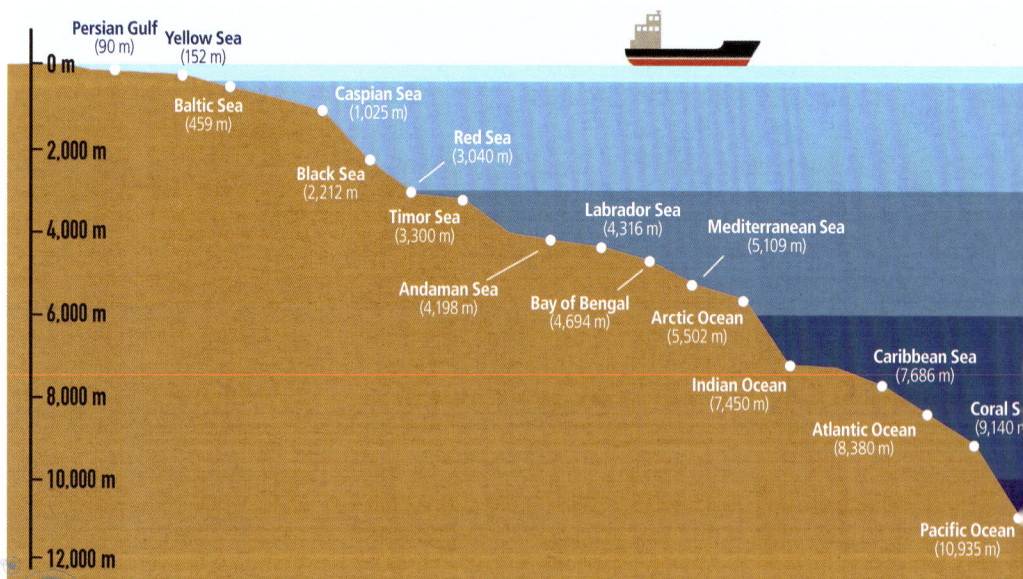

Sea and Ocean Deepest Depths

Persian Gulf (90 m)
Yellow Sea (152 m)
0 m
Baltic Sea (459 m)
Caspian Sea (1,025 m)
2,000 m
Red Sea (3,040 m)
Black Sea (2,212 m)
Timor Sea (3,300 m)
Labrador Sea (4,316 m)
4,000 m
Andaman Sea (4,198 m)
Bay of Bengal (4,694 m)
Mediterranean Sea (5,109 m)
Arctic Ocean (5,502 m)
6,000 m
Caribbean Sea (7,686 m)
Indian Ocean (7,450 m)
8,000 m
Atlantic Ocean (8,380 m)
Coral S (9,140 r)
10,000 m
Pacific Ocean (10,935 m)
12,000 m

Deepest Known Creature

Scientists discovered a snailfish swimming 8,178 m (26,832 ft.) below sea level. These pink, slimy fish are about 22.6 centimeters (8.9 inches) long. Their skulls have evolved to withstand the incredible water pressure at that depth.

snailfish

Rattail fish have large eyes that help them detect even the faintest amounts of light.

The farther away the water's surface is, the less food and light are available. However, life finds a way to exist in these depths. Animals that can stand the pressure include certain octopuses, sharks, rattail fish, and angler fish. Countless **microscopic** creatures survive there, too. And many creatures, such as sea cucumbers, can create their own light. This is done through a chemical reaction in their cells.

Studying Marine Life

Scientists study the oceans and marine life for many reasons. Scientists can learn about the **adaptations** of deep-sea creatures and how species in the oceans live. Learning about the oceans can also teach us to better manage the resources they provide. That helps us make sure they are still around for future generations. Finally, the oceans can reveal new plant and animal species.

What else can the oceans teach us? We won't know unless we explore them. But the deepest parts of oceans are distant, alien worlds. They are very hard to explore. This is where underwater vehicles come in. They allow people to safely explore the depths.

The world's first submarine was created by a Dutch inventor named Cornelis Drebbel in 1620. It was a rowboat that was covered with greased leather to seal it against the water. Tubes that went up to the surface provided air. Drebbel used it to dive about 3.7 to 4.6 m (12 to 15 ft.) below a river's surface.

Submarine technology has come a long way since then. Since the late nineteenth century, motor-powered submarines have been navigating the seas. Today, scientists use a variety of technologically advanced underwater vehicles to help them explore the deepest parts of the oceans.

reconstruction of Drebbel's submarine in England

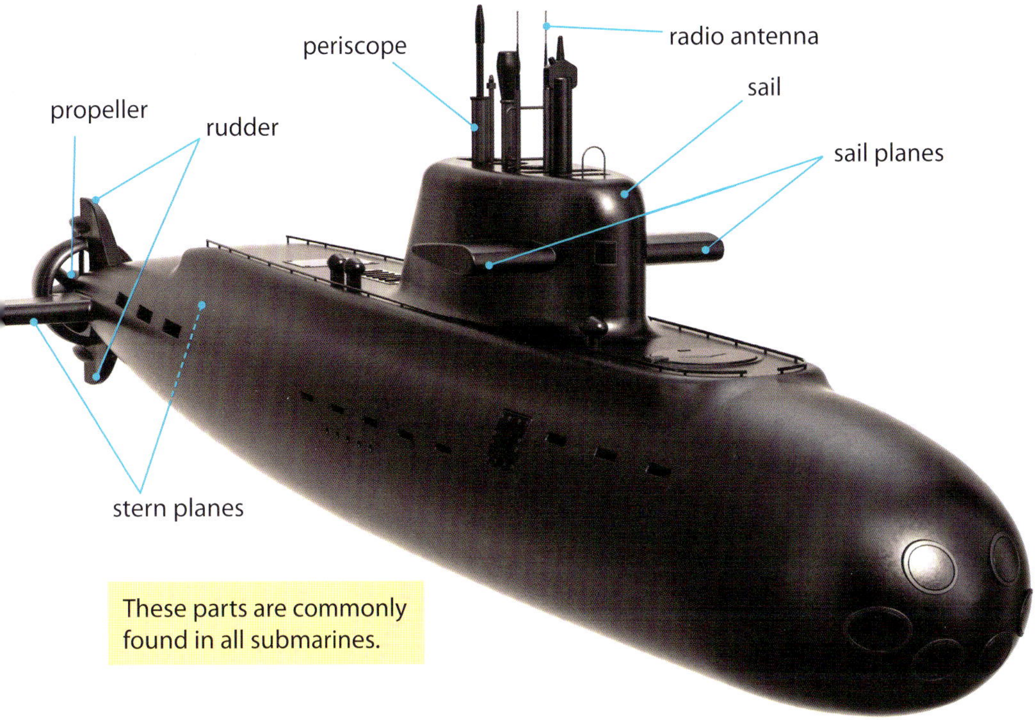

propeller

rudder

periscope

radio antenna

sail

sail planes

stern planes

These parts are commonly found in all submarines.

Seaweed Savior?

ENGINEERING

Scientists in Iceland are growing seaweed on buoys in the ocean. They think it might help fight **climate change**. That's because seaweed absorbs carbon from the atmosphere. Eventually, the buoys will be sunk to the seafloor. If everything goes according to plan, the carbon will be stored underwater for at least 800 years!

Underwater Vehicles

The underwater vehicles scientists use fall into three categories. Each type of vehicle is important for ocean research. Together, they form a super-useful toolkit.

Human-Occupied Vehicles (HOVs) carry a crew of scientists beneath the water's surface. These vehicles are used when scientists want to directly observe or work on something. They can collect samples and conduct experiments in real-time. This ability sets HOVs apart from other underwater vehicles.

Remotely Operated Vehicles (ROVs) are uncrewed, and scientists operate them from the surface. These vehicles are best for very precise tasks. They're also good in situations that require **endurance** and an extended time underwater. For example, they can collect samples from extreme depths or steer through tricky terrain. All the while, they provide a continuous stream of **data** and imagery.

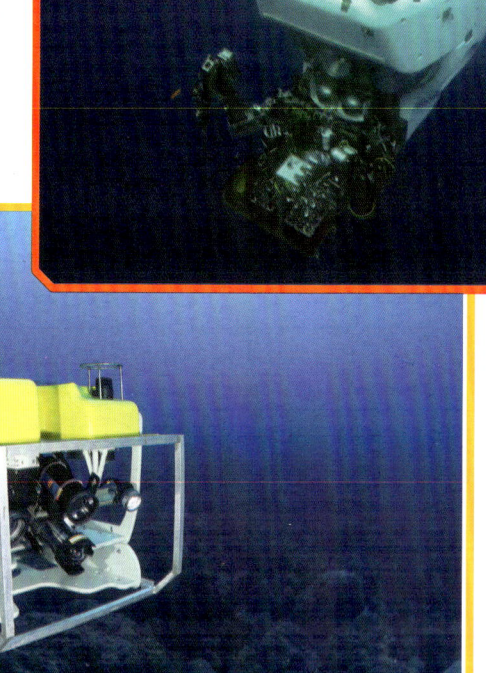

Human-Occupied Vehicle

Remotely Operated Vehicle

ARTS

Film Director in the Abyss

In 1989, film director James Cameron released the film *The Abyss*. It explores the challenges of deep-sea exploration and run-ins with unknown marine creatures. In 2012, he furthered his love of deep-sea exploration. He piloted a solo submarine trip nearly 11.3 km (7 mi.) underwater!

Autonomous Underwater Vehicles (AUVs) are also uncrewed. But unlike ROVs, they are not directly controlled by humans. Instead, they go on preprogrammed missions. These vehicles can cover large areas efficiently. That makes them best for jobs like mapping the seafloor. Plus, they stay on task for a long time without any help from people. They are a cost-effective way to gather huge amounts of data.

Autonomous Underwater Vehicle

Seeing What Can't Be Seen

Most underwater vehicles have lights that scientists use to see in the dark. But some vehicles have another way of seeing: sonar. *Sonar* is a shortened word for "sound navigation and ranging." This technology uses sound waves to find the locations of objects. First, a part called a **transducer** sends out sound waves into the water. The sound waves hit any objects and bounce back as echoes. Then, the echoes are sent to a display where scientists can see them on a screen. Scientists study these echoes for many purposes.

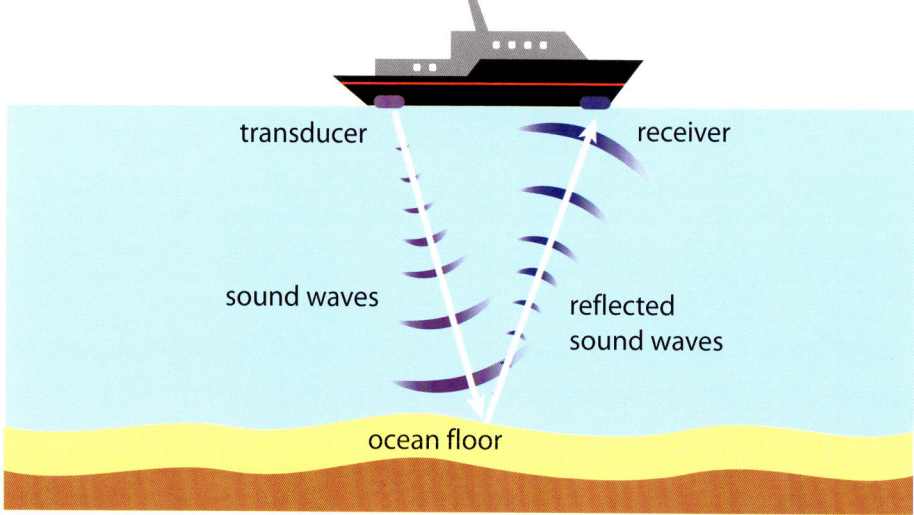

transducer

receiver

sound waves

reflected sound waves

ocean floor

TECHNOLOGY

Shipwreck Site

In 1912, a luxury cruise ship called the *Titanic* sank in the ocean. In 1985, scientists used sonar to locate the remains of the sunken ship. A ROV called *Argo* was used to find the *Titanic*. *Argo* was equipped with various sensors, including sonar sensors. *Argo* sent detailed sonar images of the shipwreck's location to scientists working on the surface.

Argo

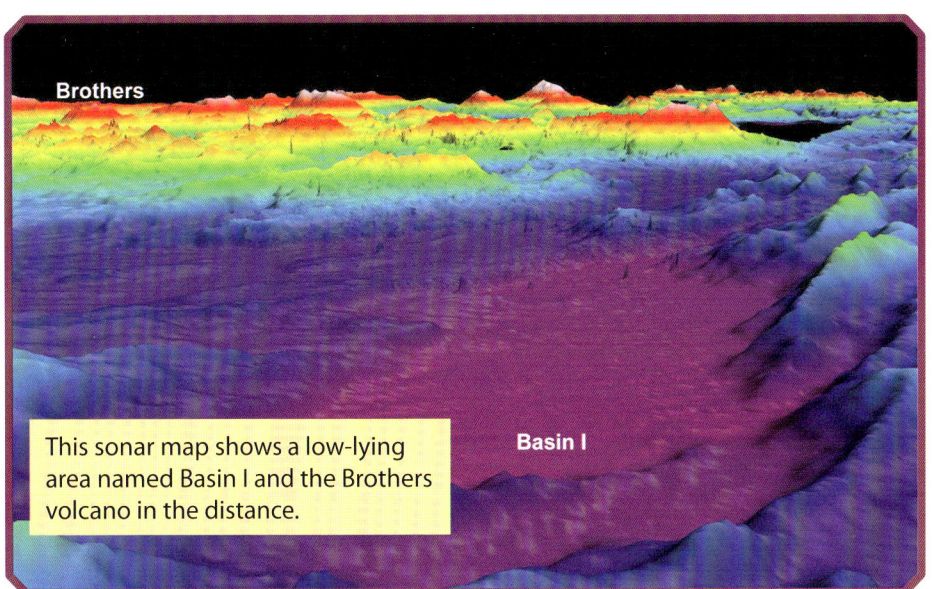

Brothers

Basin I

This sonar map shows a low-lying area named Basin I and the Brothers volcano in the distance.

Scientists have used sonar to map the seafloor. Ships or submarines send sound waves deep into the ocean. The returning echoes help create precise maps. The transducer can determine the range of objects based on how long the echoes take to bounce back. Maps created with sonar can show undersea mountains, volcanoes, valleys, and other features. These maps help scientists understand what Earth's crust looks like. They also help scientists understand ocean activity. That includes factors such as currents, tides, and temperature variations.

Scientists also use sonar to study marine life. Scientists use AUVs that have sonar to track the behavior of marine animals. For instance, researchers use sonar to study the **migration** patterns of whales. Sonar data provides insights into the whales' behavior and how they travel. This helps scientists protect them and their **habitats**.

Deep-Sea Corals

When you think of ocean corals, you probably think of shallow-water species. These corals are colorful and beautiful—and important. One-quarter of all ocean species depend on coral reefs for food and shelter. That's why corals are known as the rainforests of the sea.

What might surprise you is that corals also live in the deepest parts of the ocean. Scientists have discovered almost as many deep-sea corals as they have shallow-water corals. Deep-sea corals do not need to depend on sunlight to survive. Instead, they get **nutrients** by trapping tiny organisms from passing ocean currents. These corals can also thrive in the coldest ocean water. They have even been found off the icy coast of Antarctica.

As recently as the turn of the century, scientists did not know very much about the existence of deep-sea corals. They didn't know where these corals could be found. But in the last 20 years, they have learned a lot. For example, they have discovered more than 3,300 species of deep-sea corals.

How have scientists learned all this new information about deep-sea corals? You guessed it—submarines and sonar. Both technologies have unlocked many mysteries about these marine organisms.

FUN FACT

Some species of deep-sea corals glow in the dark! This ability helps them attract prey, which are drawn in by the light. Scientists also think that this ability may serve as a form of communication among corals.

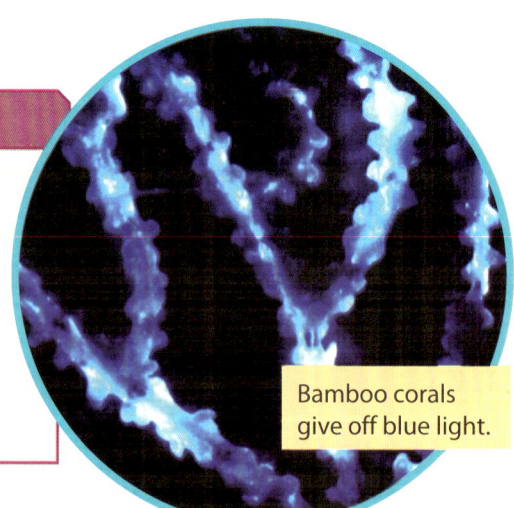

Bamboo corals give off blue light.

These three deep-sea corals are all octocorals, meaning they each have eight tentacles and are soft rather than hard corals.

Studying Corals

Underwater vehicles are the key to studying deep-sea corals. These vehicles are used to help create 3D maps of the seafloor. To do this, the vehicles are equipped with sonar devices. The devices are put into watertight shells that are mounted on the vehicles. Then, the devices send pulses of sound waves into the water. Computers measure how long it takes for the sound waves to travel to the seafloor and bounce back. All these measurements are put together into one image. Colors are used to show different depths. In this way, sonar can create colorful maps of the seafloor.

Scientists use these maps to pinpoint areas where deep-sea corals might be found. Then, they can figure out where to do additional research. The sonar maps also provide information about the conditions where these corals live, which is useful to scientists.

A scientist studies a color-coded map of the seafloor's depths, looking for coral sites.

Deep Discoverer, a ROV, takes photos and videos of bamboo corals off the coast of Massachusetts.

Underwater vehicles allow scientists to learn about the most remote deep-sea coral habitats. Some of these vehicles are HOVs, like the *Pisces V*. Scientists use this vehicle to study the waters around the Hawaiian Islands. But HOVs can also travel deep into the oceans. Once there, scientists can observe deep-sea corals in person. With ROVs and AUVs, scientists can study regions that they couldn't reach otherwise.

These vehicles have underwater cameras. They take close-up photos of deep-sea corals. Super-precise robotic arms on these vehicles can collect samples of water, coral, and more. When these vehicles return to the surface, scientists study the samples in a lab.

FUN FACT

Deep-sea corals and sponges can live for thousands of years. Scientists have found a black coral that was more than 4,250 years old. The oldest sponge ever found is estimated to be between 11,000 and 13,000 years old!

black coral

Identifying Threats

With sonar and submarines, scientists have learned about many threats to deep-sea corals. For starters, the rise in **carbon dioxide** levels in oceans is a big threat. These increased levels are a result of human pollution. Higher levels of this gas cause the oceans to become more acidic at a fast pace. If the water has too much acid, it can weaken the skeletons of corals.

Warm water is a huge threat to corals. And the temperature of ocean waters is rising due to the use of **fossil fuels**. This increased warmth causes the algae that live on coral to die out. Corals depend on algae for food. As colorful algae disappear, corals are left ghostly white. This is called *coral bleaching*. While corals can survive in this state, they are at higher risk of death. Sometimes, only a section of a coral will become bleached while the rest of it remains healthy.

Bleached coral (white) is surrounded by healthy coral (brown).

Humans affect the health of corals in other ways, too. **Overfishing** of corals disrupts reefs. Boat anchors and divers can scar reefs if they get too close. Plus, some sunscreens that wash off swimmers' bodies are also harmful.

The good news is that scientists keep learning more about these threats. They spread the word about protecting corals. As a result, some countries have passed laws to create protected areas. In these waters, fishing and boating activities are not allowed.

An abandoned anchor chain from a boat damaged the corals it fell on.

MATHEMATICS

Rising Ocean Temperatures

Before gas engines were invented, average global sea temperatures were lower. But the average global temperature has been steadily rising. Scientists have discovered that ocean temperatures rise 0.28 °C (0.5 °F) every decade.

Humans Make Noisy Neighbors

Humans use sonar to create maps that help them navigate oceans. Did you know that some animals use sound waves to locate objects, too? For example, bats use a process called **_echolocation_** to guide them and locate food as they fly in the dark. Certain ocean mammals do the same thing.

Imagine a pod of dolphins swimming gracefully through the ocean. As they swim, they make clicking sounds. These sound waves spread out into the water and bounce back when they hit an object. Dolphins receive these sound waves, which travel into their brains so they can interpret the sounds as images. In a way, this allows dolphins to "see" with their ears. One of the main reasons why dolphins use echolocation is to find food. Their clicks bounce off fish or other prey in the water. This allows dolphins to know exactly where to catch their next meals.

Dolphins work together in their pods to find schools of fish to eat.

FUN FACT

Blue whales can create intense, low-frequency sounds. These sounds can travel for thousands of kilometers. This is one of the longest-distance communication methods in the animal kingdom!

Like dolphins, whales use echolocation for their daily tasks. Whales produce clicks and sounds that serve useful purposes. They use echolocation to find food and communicate with others. Whales create patterns of clicks and calls to send messages to other whales in their pods. This helps them stay connected with their families and communities in the vast ocean. Whales also use echolocation to navigate through the water. Using their clicks and other sounds, they can detect the seafloor and other obstacles. This ensures safe travels during their long migrations or daily movements.

Echolocation Process

Whales send sound waves into the water.

Sound waves bounce off objects and return as echoes to whales, allowing whales to sense the objects' locations.

Human Effects

For animals that depend on echolocation to survive, human activity can be a real problem. Extra noise caused by humans disrupts the life of marine animals. Large container ships make a constant hum as they travel, which drowns out whale calls. Stress from human sounds can also affect seals, tuna, and oysters.

Military use of sonar is known to cause beaked whales to **ascend** rapidly. They try to escape from the sonar pulses. However, ascending too fast can cause dangerous blood clots in the whales. And some of these whales have stranded themselves on beaches after surfacing.

U.S. Navy ship

In the mid-2000s, scientists wanted to learn more about this behavior. They knew that beaked whales are a deep-diving species. They were likely to be in deep canyons below areas where the U.S. Navy conducted training exercises. And sonar was used as a part of those exercises. Scientists figured out that the echoes from the sonar might be bouncing around the canyons, deeply affecting the whales.

Scientists wanted to know exactly what happened to whales when they encountered sonar. So, they developed a plan for safely testing sonar sounds on marine animals. They first went to a Navy training range in the Bahamas. There, scientists used the Navy's high-tech tools to find and track beaked whales. Scientists tagged the whales with suction-cup listening devices. Then, they played simulated sonar sounds to the whales and listened to their responses. As they expected, beaked whales had negative reactions.

Beaked whales are named for their beak-like mouths which make them look similar to many species of dolphins.

Testing Results

Scientists worked on this project for two years in the Bahamas and one year in the Mediterranean Sea. They tracked the responses of several types of whales as well as seals. Then, they went to the coast of California. They focused on the waters around a U.S. Navy training range near San Clemente Island. There, they monitored 21 species of whales, dolphins, seals, and sea lions.

Of all the animals scientists tested, they found that beaked whales were the most sensitive to the sounds. Blue whales, on the other hand, showed almost no reaction. While other mammals tried to avoid the sounds, they did not change their behavior patterns. All this data confirmed scientists' original theories that sonar negatively affected beaked whales.

Cargo ships like this one can hold thousands of containers' worth of goods.

Years later, scientists collected more evidence that human noise stresses out whales. Researchers tested samples of whale feces during the COVID-19 pandemic. During the early stages of the pandemic, cargo ships were mostly stopped from traveling. Compared to samples from earlier and busier times, the COVID-19 samples showed a big drop in stress hormones. Scientists learned that whales were less stressed when there were fewer ships in the oceans.

Scientists have more work to do, but these findings help them better understand ocean mammals. The more they learn, the better they will know how to protect and conserve these animals.

Researching a Better Future

Sonar and submarine technology continues to advance in exciting ways. New projects help scientists learn more about the ocean. For example, scientists have trained teams of sonar-equipped AUVs to work together. These vehicles act like packs of animals in the wild. They communicate with one another and learn as they collect data. This allows them to make decisions about where to go. They produce detailed seafloor maps quickly and efficiently.

Scientists are also developing smaller, more portable sonar sensors. These are used on AUVs. Smaller sensors make these vehicles easier to maneuver. It allows them to collect data in areas that larger vehicles can't access.

However, advances are not all about AUVs. New, super-light **ultrasound** sonar devices are coming soon. They will help humans communicate underwater. Since traditional radio does not travel well in water, communication is difficult. But these new devices use ultrasound sonar. They will allow people to judge distances, find obstacles, and communicate in a similar way to dolphins and other sea mammals. They can even be used to communicate through objects, such as steel.

Oceans make up the vast majority of Earth's living space. Scientists are using underwater vehicles and sonar to learn more about them every day. The hope is that these cutting-edge tools can help people preserve them.

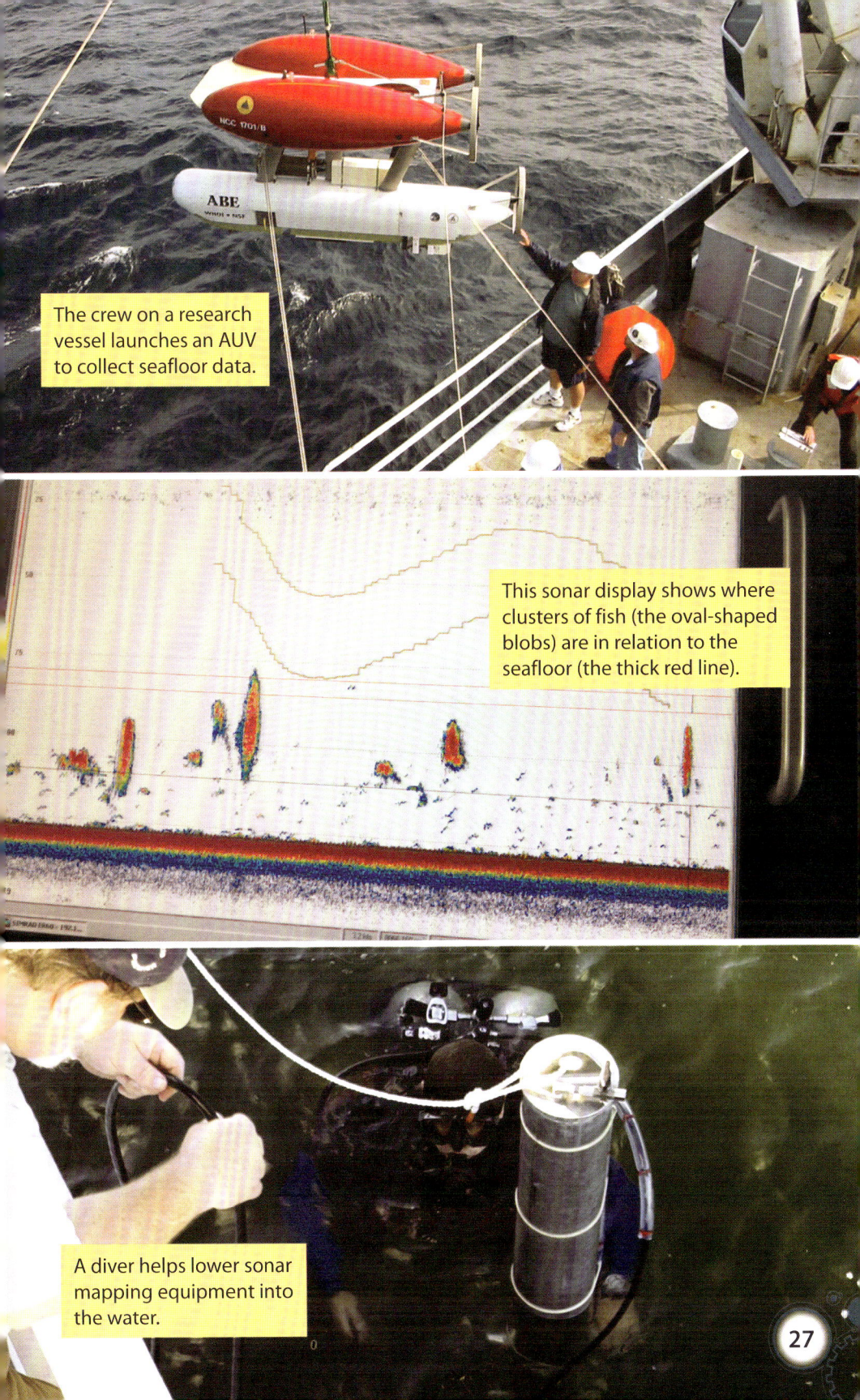

The crew on a research vessel launches an AUV to collect seafloor data.

This sonar display shows where clusters of fish (the oval-shaped blobs) are in relation to the seafloor (the thick red line).

A diver helps lower sonar mapping equipment into the water.

STEAM CHALLENGE

Define the Problem

Submarines travel throughout the oceans, sinking and rising to different depths. But their engines can have a negative effect on marine life due to the sound waves they create. So, marine biologists are partnering with naval architects to address this problem. They want to create a new protective material that can be used to make submarines. They want this material to help reduce engine sound waves from bouncing off submarines and spreading. Now, they've asked you to test your ideas for a sound-reducing submarine.

 **Constraints:** You may only use the materials that are provided for you.

 **Criteria:** Your submarine must be large enough to fit a cell phone inside but small enough to carry in your hands. The submarine must open and close.

Research and Brainstorm

What is amplitude, and how is it measured? How can sound waves be reflected, absorbed, and transmitted through various materials? What types of materials help reflect or absorb these waves the best? How can your design reduce sound waves to prevent them from reaching the exterior?

Design and Build

Sketch two designs for your sound-reducing submarine. Be sure to label the materials you intend to use. Partner with a small group of classmates to share your ideas. Then, design and build a final submarine that incorporates everyone's ideas.

Test and Improve

Play a song on a cell phone, turning the volume up all the way. Then, put the cell phone inside your submarine and close the opening. Using a laptop or tablet, go to a sound level meter website. Test all four sides of your submarine, recording the decibel reading at each location by setting the laptop or tablet 30 centimeters (12 inches) from the submarine. How can you reduce the noise even more? Modify your design, rebuild it, and test your second prototype with the same sound level check.

Reflect and Share

How did your knowledge of sound waves help you when constructing your model? What part of the process did you enjoy the most during this challenge? Was anything difficult for you and your group? How did you overcome it?

Glossary

adaptations—the ways living organisms change over time to better survive in their environments

ascend—to go up or climb

autonomous—capable of controlling itself without outside help (like from humans)

carbon dioxide—a colorless, odorless gas that is produced by burning carbon and organic compounds; contributes to global climate change

climate change—the ongoing increase in average global temperatures that affects Earth's climate

corals—marine invertebrates that live in colonies as individual polyps or as reefs

data—facts and statistics collected to be studied

deployed—used for a specific purpose

echolocation—a process for locating distant or invisible objects by sound waves reflected back to the animal from the objects

endurance—the ability to sustain a prolonged stressful effort or activity

fossil fuels—fuels such as coal, oil, or natural gas that are burned for power, heat, or electricity

habitats—the natural homes or environments of animals, plants, or other organisms

marine—having to do with the sea

microscopic—only able to be seen through a microscope

migration—the movement of animals from one location to another

nutrients—substances that provide nourishment for living things

overfishing—removing a species of fish from an area by too much fishing

submarines—watercrafts that can go underwater; also known as underwater vehicles

transducer—device that converts energy from one form to another

ultrasound—sound that has a frequency above 20,000 hertz

Index

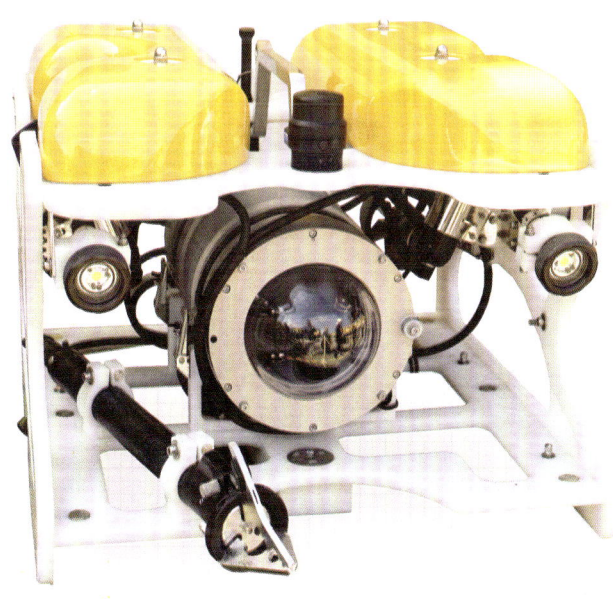

Do you want to work with sonar or submarines?

Here are some tips to keep in mind for the future.

"Read as much as you can about the ocean and its creatures. Books open up the world hidden beneath the waves. Plus, YouTube has countless wonderful documentaries that inspire a passion in the oceans."

– Dr. Jonathan Cybulski, Postdoctoral Researcher, Smithsonian Tropical Research Institute

"Explore how submarines work by building your own models using plastic bottles. Sonar calculates distance with reflected sound, or echoes. You can learn more about this by having fun with echoes in a large building or a cave."

– Dr. Kimberly García-Mendez, Lab Manager, Smithsonian Tropical Research Institute